Heroes *for* Civil Rights

by DAVID A. ADLER

illustrated by BILL FARNSWORTH

HOLIDAY HOUSE / New York

Introduction

The Thirteenth Amendment to the U.S. Constitution, which was adopted in 1865, ended slavery in the United States; but its passage did not bring true equal rights for African Americans. Many restrictive laws, known as Jim Crow laws, were passed to keep blacks and whites separate. Even the name Jim Crow, taken from a character in minstrel shows who acted in a foolish slapstick parody of blacks, was an affront.

In 1892, Homer Plessy, a man with an African-American great-grandmother, decided to challenge such laws. He sat in a Louisiana "whites only" railroad car and told the conductor he was black. Homer Plessy was arrested and jailed. His case went all the way to the U.S. Supreme Court, which declared in 1896 that trains with "whites only" and "colored only" cars, so-called "separate but equal" facilities, were *legal*. This decision in favor of Jim Crow led to separate schools for blacks and whites, separate train cars, parks, waiting rooms, telephone booths, ambulances, and restrooms; and separate sections on buses, in hospitals, and in theaters. These were not the only restrictions faced by African Americans. In many places, literacy tests and poll taxes prevented African Americans from voting.

In 1910, the National Association for the Advancement of Colored People, the NAACP, was founded and began a long battle against segregation. There were many defeats and some victories. In 1954, in the landmark case of *Brown v. Board of Education*, the Supreme Court ruled that separate facilities could not be equal, that to separate races was to declare them unequal. Despite the ruling, segregation persisted. The courageous people profiled here are just a few of the many who, following that 1954 ruling, adopted nonviolence as a way to fight for the civil rights of all U.S. citizens.

For my cousins, Leah and Mark Adler
D. A. A.

To Regina
B. F.

Text copyright © 2008 by David A. Adler
Illustrations copyright © 2008 by Bill Farnsworth
All Rights Reserved
Printed and Bound in Malaysia
The text typeface is Celestia Antiqua.
The artwork was created with oil paint on canvas.
www.holidayhouse.com
First Edition
1 3 5 7 9 10 8 6 4 2

Library of Congress Cataloging-in-Publication Data
Adler, David A.
Heroes for civil rights / by David A. Adler ; illustrated by Bill Farnsworth.—1st ed.
p. cm.
Includes bibliographical references.
ISBN-13: 978-0-8234-2008-7 (hardcover)
1. African-American civil rights workers—Biography—Juvenile literature.
2. Civil rights workers—United States—Biography—Juvenile literature.
3. African Americans—Civil rights—History—Juvenile literature.
4. Civil rights movements—United States—History—Juvenile literature.
I. Farnsworth, Bill. II. Title.
E185.96.A424 2007
323.092'273—dc22
2006038185

Contents

Ralph Abernathy
(1926–1990)

Early Monday morning, December 5, 1955, the Reverend Ralph Abernathy watched from his house in Montgomery, Alabama, as the first public bus of the day went past. "There were no passengers," Abernathy later remembered. "The boycott was working—it was working perfectly."

The bus boycott had been organized by Abernathy, Dr. Martin Luther King, Jr., and others to protest Montgomery's segregated buses. They wanted to show the bus company that African Americans would no longer accept being treated as second-class citizens. The boycott would last for more than a year and bring an early victory to the civil rights movement. It demonstrated the power of nonviolent protest.

Abernathy led marches to gain voting rights and fair treatment for African Americans in Selma and Birmingham, Alabama; Albany, Georgia; and Washington, D.C.

"There will be no slowing up; there will be no turning back," he said in 1960. "There will be no turning to hatred, bitterness, or violence. . . . Our goal: first-class citizenship. Our method: love and nonviolence. We want freedom now. . . . We must prepare ourselves for suffering. Some of us may give our very lives."

Together with his friend Dr. King, Abernathy helped found the civil rights movement. He was there when Dr. King was shot and killed. After King's murder, Abernathy continued their work. "You can kill the dreamer," he said, "but you cannot kill the dream."

Medgar Evers
(1925–1963)

"In the first grade, white kids in their school buses would throw things at us," Medgar Evers said in 1962. "When I was eleven or twelve, a close friend of the family got lynched. . . . I began wondering how long I could stand it."

Evers was an American soldier during World War II. He served in France and Germany; but in 1946, when he came home to Mississippi, he and other African Americans heard that they would not be allowed to vote. "Word had gone out," he later said, "that we weren't to come to town on Election Day." Evers and a few others went anyway. "About fifteen or twenty white men with knives and guns were ready for us. . . . Now after the Germans and the Japanese hadn't killed us, it looked as though the white Mississippians would."

Evers was angry. He became a leader of the Mississippi chapter of the NAACP (National Association for the Advancement of Colored People). He led meetings, marches, and boycotts for the civil rights of African Americans. He worked to integrate schools in Mississippi. Some people answered his call for change with threats and violence. Evers's house was firebombed. He was beaten and chased.

On June 12, 1963, when Medgar Evers returned home from a church meeting, a hidden gunman shot him and ran. Evers fell at the door to his house and died a short while later.

"Surely there can be some solace," President John F. Kennedy wrote to Evers's wife, Myrlie, "in the realization of the justice of the cause for which your husband gave his life."

Andrew Goodman (1943–1964)
James Earl Chaney (1943–1964)
Michael Henry Schwerner (1939–1964)

During the early 1960s, in some southern states, few African Americans were able to vote. Unfair rules and threats kept them from the polls. In June 1964 several civil rights groups in Mississippi launched Freedom Summer, a huge effort throughout the state to get African Americans registered to vote in time for the coming presidential election. Hundreds of people, many of them white college students from the Northeast, joined the drive.

"We will be ready for them," the white mayor of Jackson, Mississippi, declared.

On June 20, the first volunteers arrived in Mississippi. By the next day one of them, Andrew Goodman of New York, was missing, along with two civil rights workers, James Chaney and Michael Schwerner.

FBI agents were sent to investigate, but it wasn't until forty-four days later, on August 4, that their bodies were found in a station wagon, a bullet in each of them. James Chaney, who was black, had also been severely beaten.

"As I stand here, I not only blame the people who pulled the trigger," David Dennis, a civil rights worker, said at Chaney's funeral. He blamed local and national leaders who let segregation go on for so long. "One hundred years ago, if the proper thing had been done," he said, "we wouldn't be here today mourning the death of a brave young man like James Chaney."

Twenty-one men, including a sheriff and deputy sheriff, were arrested for the killings, but the charges were quickly dropped. Later, six of the men were jailed on lesser charges.

THE GREENSBORO FOUR
Ezell Blair, Jr. (now Jibreel Khazan) (1941–),
Franklin McCain (1941–),
Joseph McNeil (1942–), and
David Richmond (1941–1990)

On February 1, 1960, four freshmen from an all-black Greensboro, North Carolina, college entered a downtown F. W. Woolworth store. Joseph McNeil and Franklin McCain bought toothpaste and school supplies. Then, along with their friends Ezell Blair and David Richmond, they sat at the lunch counter, asked to be served, and were refused. "We don't serve colored here," the white waitress told them.

"Why is it that you serve me at one counter and deny me at another?" McCain asked.

There was no real answer to McCain's question, and the four students sat there, unserved until the store closed. While they were there, an elderly white woman offered support. She told McNeil, "I'm disappointed that this took you so long."

This peaceful protest spread. There were sit-ins at lunch counters in many other cities. The young protesters were insulted, cursed, spit on, and hit. People blew smoke in their faces, ground cigarettes on their backs, spilled soda and ketchup on them, and pulled them off their stools. But the students refused to fight back. In Nashville, Tennessee, as soon as police arrested eighty students sitting at a counter, eighty others took their seats. And when the second eighty were arrested, a third group took over.

"I felt as though I had gained my manhood," McCain said of the sit-ins, "not only gained it, but had developed quite a lot of respect for it."

He and others gained victory too. In March 1960, four African Americans were served at a previously whites-only lunch counter in a Nashville bus terminal. By that summer African Americans were served at the counter in Greensboro too.

Fannie Lou Hamer
(1917–1977)

"You don't run away from problems," Fannie Lou Hamer said in 1964. "You just face them."

Fannie Lou Hamer was born and raised in Mississippi, the youngest of her parents' twenty children. In 1962, she attended her first civil rights rally, where, she later said, "they talked about how it was our rights as human beings to register and vote. I never knew we could vote. Nobody ever told us."

The next day she and seventeen others tried to register to vote and were turned away. The police arrested and jailed them, because, they said, the bus they came in was too yellow.

After she became active in the civil rights movement, Fannie Lou Hamer lost her home and job. But she continued the fight. She was cursed, beaten, and shot at. "Is this America?" Fannie Lou Hamer asked again and again. "Is this America?"

Because Mississippi's all-white delegation to the Democratic National Convention did not represent the many blacks of the state who were not allowed to vote, Hamer helped found the Mississippi Freedom Democratic Party (MFDP). At the 1964 Democratic convention, it challenged the regular state delegates for seats. The MFDP and the all-white Mississippi delegation rejected a compromise that would give the Freedom Party two seats. Nonetheless, Hamer's passionate televised appearance brought national attention to her cause. The Democratic Party resolved that at future conventions, no delegation would be recognized if anyone in its state was illegally kept from voting. The next year, the Voting Rights Act of 1965 was passed.

Hamer said she pitied people whose judgment was clouded by prejudice. "I feel sorry for anybody that could let hate wrap them up," she said. "Hate will not only destroy us. It will destroy them."

Lyndon Baines Johnson
(1908–1973)

Lyndon B. Johnson of Texas served first in the U.S. House of Representatives and then in the U.S. Senate, spending twenty-four years in Congress. In 1960, he was elected vice president of the United States. After the assassination of John F. Kennedy in 1963, he became president.

"I want to be the president," Johnson said in 1965, "who protected the right of every citizen to vote in every election. I want to be the president who helped end the hatred among his fellow men and who promoted love among people of all races, all regions, and all parties."

In many ways Lyndon Johnson did become that president.

Understanding the workings of Congress, Johnson pushed through the Civil Rights Act of 1964, which outlawed discrimination in the workplace, polls, hotels, and other public places. The next year, he pushed through the Voting Rights Act of 1965. "His brilliant leadership," Senator Edward Kennedy said of Johnson's work on these laws, "earned him a place in the history of civil rights alongside Abraham Lincoln."

"He did not just mouth the words of equality," Justice Thurgood Marshall said of President Johnson. "He put them into action."

Martin Luther King, Jr.
(1929–1968)

Dr. Martin Luther King, Jr., devoted his life to the civil rights movement. He worked tirelessly to fulfill his hopes and dreams for America, that one day his country would be free of prejudice and bigotry, that it would offer equal opportunities to all people. His first civil rights leadership role, in the Montgomery bus boycott, proved to be a test of his belief that change could come without violence. "We must use the weapon of love," he told his followers. "We must have compassion and understanding for those who hate us."

King led peaceful protests against the institution of whites-only water fountains, lunch counters, waiting rooms, and restrooms. He was a leader of the celebrated March on Washington in 1963, in which 250,000 people demonstrated peaceably for civil rights. It was there that he spoke of his dream of an American nation without prejudice.

King was threatened, hit, kicked, stabbed, and arrested and jailed. His house was firebombed, and crosses were burned on his lawn; but he never lost his faith in the power of truth and love.

In 1964, Dr. King was awarded the Nobel Peace Prize, as the "first person in the Western world to have shown us that a struggle can be waged without violence." He accepted it, he said, for "all men who love peace and brotherhood."

In March 1968, King went to Memphis, Tennessee, to demand that white and black sanitation workers get the same pay for the same work. On April 4, he stood on a balcony outside his motel room. James Earl Ray stood with a rifle in a nearby house, by an open window. He shot and killed Dr. King.

Dr. Martin Luther King, Jr., an eloquent voice for freedom, justice, and American values, had been stilled.

"Say that I was a drum major for justice," Dr. King told his congregation just two months earlier. "Say that I was a drum major for peace. I was a drum major for righteousness."

THE LITTLE ROCK NINE
Minnijean Brown (1941–), Elizabeth Eckford (1941–), Ernest Green (1941–), Thelma Mothershed (1940–), Melba Pattillo (1941–), Gloria Ray (1942–), Terrence Roberts (1941–), Jefferson Thomas (1942–), and Carlotta Walls (1942–)

September 2, 1957, the first day of the school year in Little Rock, Arkansas, was the first day of the scheduled integration of Central High School by nine African-American students.

"What I felt inside was a terrible, wrenching fear," Melba Pattillo, one of the nine, said later. She was only fifteen!

In front was a mob of angry whites and Arkansas National Guardsmen armed with guns, bayonets, and billy clubs. They prevented the black teenagers from entering the school.

"What upset me," Thelma Mothershed said at the time, "were the troops. They made no attempt to let us in. They blocked our way." But, she added, "We haven't given up."

"There is a principle involved," Mothershed's mother said. "If our boys and girls enter the white school now it will be easier for others to get in later."

Three weeks later, federal troops surrounded the school. That day the nine black students were able to go in safely.

In May 1958, Ernest Green was the first of the nine to graduate from Central High. The Little Rock Nine and their families, Green said later, "opened the eyes of many other blacks in this country to the fact that discrimination would have to be fought . . . be fought and beaten."

In 1999, each of the Little Rock Nine was awarded a Congressional Gold Medal because, President Bill Clinton said, "they paid the price."

Thurgood Marshall
(1908–1993)

Thurgood Marshall was born in Baltimore, Maryland. He was named after his grandfather, a freed slave who served in the Union army during the Civil War. Marshall's parents, a waiter and a schoolteacher, believed in hard work and the value of a good education. When Thurgood Marshall entered Howard University School of Law, his mother sold her wedding and engagement rings to help pay his expenses.

Soon after Marshall became a lawyer, he joined the legal staff of the National Association for the Advancement of Colored People, the NAACP. In 1935, he had his first victory against segregation, winning a decision that allowed an African American to enter the University of Maryland School of Law. In 1940, he argued the first of thirty-two cases before the highest court in the country, the U.S. Supreme Court. He won all but three!

Beginning in 1952, Thurgood Marshall argued in *Brown v. Board of Education*, a case that challenged school segregation. At issue was the Fourteenth Amendment to the U.S. Constitution, which guarantees each citizen "equal protection of the laws." Marshall told the Court that separate schools for blacks and whites could not be equal. "Equal," he said, "means getting the same thing, at the same time, and in the same place."

On Monday, May 17, 1954, the Supreme Court ruled "that in the field of public education the doctrine of 'separate but equal' has no place." Thurgood Marshall's arguments opened the door to true equality.

In 1967, President Lyndon Johnson appointed Marshall as a justice of the Supreme Court, the first African American ever to sit on that bench.

"He is a man who sees the world exactly as it is," fellow justice Sandra Day O'Connor said of him, "and pushes on it to make it what it can become." She called him a "true American hero."

James Meredith
(1933–)

In 1960, when James Meredith returned from ten years of service in the U.S. Air Force, he enrolled in Jackson State College. Soon he applied for a transfer to what he considered a better school, the all-white University of Mississippi—"Ole Miss." His grades were good enough, but because he was black it took a U.S. Supreme Court ruling to get him admitted.

On September 30, 1962, Meredith arrived at Ole Miss accompanied by hundreds of federal marshals and lawyers from the U.S. Justice Department. That day, many students threw eggs, rocks, and bottles, turned over cars, and set fires. Meredith was safe in his room, but almost four hundred people were hurt. Two were killed.

Despite his tragic welcome to the school, Meredith remained. At an award ceremony the next year, New York City mayor Robert Wagner praised his courage. "In terms of unbelievable tension and danger and finally in terms of unlimited dedication, James Meredith must be given a mark second to none."

"I'm only a part of the mainstream," Meredith responded. He reminded those at the ceremony that for generations, African Americans had been fighting for their rights.

In August 1963, Meredith became the first African American to graduate from Ole Miss. "We live in a difficult time," the Reverend William Arthur Pennington said at the graduation ceremony. He prayed for "unity out of discord, love out of hate, hope out of despair."

Rosa Parks
(1913–2005)

On December 1, 1955, Rosa Parks boarded the Cleveland Avenue bus at Court Square in Montgomery, Alabama. She paid the fare and took a seat just behind the whites-only section. At the next stops, more passengers boarded until all the front seats were taken and a white passenger was left standing.

The driver turned and told Parks and three other African Americans to get up so the white man could sit. No one got up.

"Let me have those seats!" the driver shouted.

The others moved to the back. Parks didn't.

Rosa Parks was arrested, and on December 5, she was found guilty of violating the city's segregation laws. That same day, African Americans in Montgomery refused to ride the city's buses. The bus boycott, led by Martin Luther King, Jr., Ralph Abernathy, and others, lasted for more than a year. On November 13, 1956, they had their first victory, a decision by the U.S. Supreme Court that ruled the buses must no longer have separate seating for blacks and whites. On December 21, 1956, that ruling was enforced and Rosa Parks boarded a city bus again. She took a seat in the very first row.

"She gave Dr. King the right to practice his nonviolence," said Septima Clark, a noted leader of the movement. "It was Rosa Parks who started the whole thing."

Fred Shuttlesworth
(1922–)

Fred Shuttlesworth was the pastor of a church in Birmingham, Alabama, and an active leader of the civil rights movement. In November 1956, following the Montgomery bus boycott, the U.S. Supreme Court ruled that public buses could not have separate sections for blacks and whites. Shuttlesworth declared that beginning December 26, African Americans in Birmingham would sit in the front seats of public buses, seats until then reserved for white passengers. The night before his deadline, Christmas night, a bomb was thrown into his house. His house was destroyed, but he, his wife, and children were not hurt. After the blast he was told to leave the city of Birmingham for his own safety. Shuttlesworth refused. "If the Lord could save me through this," he said, "I am here for the duration."

In 1957, when Shuttlesworth and his wife, Ruby, tried to enroll their children in an all-white Birmingham school, he was beaten and his wife was stabbed. But he didn't strike back. He helped organize boycotts of segregated public buses, sit-ins at public lunch counters where blacks were denied service, and Freedom Rides, in which black and white supporters rode together in unsegregated buses through segregated areas.

"I had the drive to get things done," Shuttlesworth once said. "Fear just didn't bother me."

"They can't kill us, can they, Daddy?" his youngest child once asked. "No, darling," he replied. "They can't kill hope."

Earl Warren
(1891–1974)

"As we justices marched into the courtroom that day," Chief Justice Earl Warren wrote later of May 17, 1954, "there was a tenseness that I have not seen equaled before or since."

Three years before, several African-American families from Topeka, Kansas, sued to have their children transferred from an all-black public school to an all-white one. The local court had ruled against them, citing an 1896 U.S. Supreme Court ruling in *Plessy v. Ferguson* that separate-but-equal facilities were acceptable. The families appealed and in 1952 were joined by people with similar cases from South Carolina, Virginia, Delaware, and Washington, D.C. This case went to the U.S. Supreme Court.

On that tense day in 1954, the Court gave its ruling.

"Does segregation of children in public schools solely on the basis of race," Warren asked when he read the Court's opinion, "deprive the children of equal opportunities? We unanimously believe that it does."

It was Justice Warren who had pulled the justices together to make the decision unanimous. Jim Crow laws had always been wrong. Now, thanks to Warren's Court, they were illegal.

"Harmony in race relations is not simply or easily achieved," Warren later wrote. "The question of racial discrimination is never settled until it is settled right."

Chronology

1953–1968

1953 The African-American community of Baton Rouge, Louisiana, boycotts the city's segregated public buses for seven days and achieves partial victory, with blacks allowed to sit in all but two front seats, June 20–24.

Supreme Court Chief Justice Fred Vinson dies suddenly. President Dwight Eisenhower nominates Earl Warren to replace him, September 30.

1954 In *Brown v. Board of Education*, the Supreme Court rules against segregation in schools, that there is no such thing as "separate but equal," that to separate according to race is "inherently unequal," May 17.

1955 On a public bus in Montgomery, Alabama, Rosa Parks refuses to give up her seat to a white passenger, a violation of a local law, and is arrested, December 1.

The Montgomery bus boycott, led by Martin Luther King, Jr., Ralph Abernathy, and others, begins, December 5.

1956 The Supreme Court rules that segregated seating on Montgomery buses is illegal, November 13. With this ruling, the bus boycott comes to a successful end, December 21.

1957 The Arkansas National Guard, under orders of the governor, blocks nine African-American students from entering Little Rock's Central High School. President Dwight Eisenhower sends in federal troops to enforce the school's integration, September.

1960 Four African-American college students in Greensboro, North Carolina, sit at a Woolworth's lunch counter restricted to whites-only and pledge to remain until they are served. This leads to sit-ins at many other segregated lunch counters, February 1.

1961 The Freedom Rides begin, an effort to integrate interstate buses, May 4.

1962 James Meredith enrolls at the University of Mississippi, September 30.

1963 Martin Luther King, Jr., leads demonstrations in Birmingham, Alabama, to protest segregation there, April–May.

Medgar Evers is murdered in Jackson, Mississippi, June 12.

About 250,000 people participate in the March on Washington. Dr. Martin Luther King, Jr., stands on the steps of the Lincoln Memorial and delivers his "I Have a Dream" speech, August 28.

1964 The Twenty-fourth Amendment, which prohibits poll taxes, a charge for voting, is ratified by the states.

Andrew Goodman, James Chaney, and Michael Schwerner, participants in Freedom Summer, are murdered in Mississippi, June 21.

The Civil Rights Act of 1964, which prohibits discrimination in employment, in public accommodations, and at the voting booth, is passed and signed by President Lyndon Johnson, July 2.

1965 Hundreds march from Selma to Montgomery, Alabama, to gain voting rights for African Americans, January–March.

The Voting Rights Act of 1965 passes Congress and is signed by President Lyndon Johnson, August 6.

1966 Edward W. Brooke is elected in Massachusetts to the U.S. Senate, the first African American to serve in the Senate since the 1880s, November.

1967 President Johnson names Thurgood Marshall to the Supreme Court, June 13.

1968 Martin Luther King, Jr., is assassinated in Memphis, Tennessee, April 4.

Source Notes

Each source note includes the first word or words and the last word or words of a quotation and its source. References are to books cited in the Selected Bibliography.

p. 5: "There were no . . . working perfectly.": Abernathy, Ralph, p. 142.
"There will be . . . our very lives.": Abernathy, Donzaleigh, p. 54.
"You can kill . . . kill the dream.": *New York Times*, April 18, 1990, p. B7.

p. 6: "In the . . . stand it.": Mendelsohn, pp. 64–65.
"Word had . . . Mississippians would.": Mendelsohn, p. 77.
"Surely . . . his life.": Mendelsohn, p. 77.

p. 9: "We will be ready for them": Williams, p. 229.
"As I stand . . . like James Chaney.": Williams, p. 239.

p. 10: "Why is it . . . at another?": Williams, p. 127.
"I'm disappointed . . . so long.": McNeil interview.
"I felt . . . respect for it.": McWhorter, p. 55.

p. 13: "You don't . . . face them.": *New York Times*,

August 24, 1964, p. 17.
"they talked . . . told us.": *New York Times*, March 15, 1977, p. 40.
"Is this America?": *New York Times*, August 21, 1964, p. 12.
"I feel sorry . . . destroy them.": *New York Times*, August 24, 1964, p. 17.

p. 15: "I want to be . . . and all parties.": *New York Times*, January 24, 1973, p. 26.
"His brilliant . . . alongside Abraham Lincoln.": *New York Times*, January 23, 1973, p. 81.
"He did . . . into action.": *New York Times*, January 24, 1973, p. 22.

p. 17: "We must . . . who hate us.": *New York Times*, April 5, 1968, p. 25.
"first person . . . without violence.": *New York Times*, April 4, 1968, p. 25.
"all men . . . and brotherhood.": *New York Times*, April 5, 1968, p. 25.
"Say that . . . for righteousness.": *New York Times*, April 7, 1968, p. 65.

p. 18: "What I felt . . . wrenching fear.": Hampton and Fayer, p. 45.
"What upset . . . given up.": *New York Times*, September 10, 1957, p. 27.
"There is . . . in later.": *New York Times*, September 10, 1957, p. 27.
"opened . . . and beaten.": *New York Times*, December 12, 1976, p. 63.
"they paid the price.": *New York Times*, November 10, 1999, p. A16.

p. 21: "Equal . . . same place.": *New York Times*, January 25, 1993, p. A1.
"that in . . . no place.": *New York Times*, May 13, 1954, p. 1.
"He is . . . can become.": *New York Times*, January 26, 1993, p. A22.
"true American hero.": *New York Times*, January 25, 1993, p. B9.

p. 22: "In terms . . . to none . . . I'm only . . . mainstream.": *New York Times*, June 1, 1963, p. 8.
"We live . . . of despair.": *New York Times*, August 19, 1963, p. 1.

p. 25: "Let me . . . seats!": Brinkley, p. 106.

"She gave . . . whole thing.": Olson, p. 130.

p. 26: "If the . . . duration.": McWhorter, p. 6.

"I had . . . bother me.": Powledge, p. 80.

"They can't . . . kill hope.": McWhorter, p. 7.

p. 29: "As we . . . or since.": Warren, p. 3.

"Does segregation . . . it does.": Warren, p. 3.

"Harmony . . . settled right.": Warren, pp. 292–293.

Selected Bibliography

Abernathy, Donzaleigh. *Partners to History: Martin Luther King Jr., Ralph David Abernathy, and the Civil Rights Movement.* New York: Crown, 2003.

Abernathy, Ralph David. *And the Walls Came Tumbling Down: An Autobiography.* New York: Harper, 1989.

Brinkley, Douglas. *Rosa Parks.* New York: Viking, 2000.

Hampton, Henry, and Steve Fayer, with Sarah Flynn. *Voices of Freedom: An Oral History of the Civil Rights Movement from the 1950s through the 1980s.* New York: Bantam, 1990.

McNeil, Joseph. Interview with author, June 16, 2005.

McWhorter, Diane. *A Dream of Freedom: The Civil Rights Movement from 1954–1968.* Scholastic: New York, 2004.

Mendelsohn, Jack. *The Martyrs: Sixteen Who Gave Their Lives for Social Justice.* New York: Harper, 1966.

New York Times, May 18, 1954; September 10, 1957; June 1, 1963; August 19, 1963; August 21, 1964; August 24, 1964; April 4–7, 1968; January 23–24, 1973; December 12, 1976; March 15, 1977; April 18, 1990; January 25–26, 1993; and November 10, 1999.

Olson, Lynne. *Freedom's Daughters: The Unsung Heroines of the Civil Rights Movement from 1830 to 1970.* New York: Scribner, 2001.

Patterson, Charles. *The Civil Rights Movement.* New York: Facts on File, 1995.

Powledge, Fred. *Free at Last? The Civil Rights Movement and the People Who Made It.* Boston: Little Brown, 1991.

Warren, Earl. *The Memoirs of Earl Warren.* New York: Doubleday, 1977.

Williams, Juan. *Eyes on the Prize: America's Civil Rights Years, 1954–1965.* New York: Viking, 1987.